REMOVED FROM COLLECTION

DATE DUE		

The WEAVERS

Early American coverlet woven in the Wheel of Fortune pattern.
This is a "summer-and-winter" weave, in which the reverse side
shows the opposite effect of the front, as the turned-over
corner here shows. Possibly it was because of this opposite
effect that the weave acquired its name, summer-and-winter.
(PHOTO: COLLECTION OF THE NEWARK MUSEUM, NEWARK, NEW JERSEY).

COLONIAL CRAFTSMEN

The
WEAVERS

WRITTEN & ILLUSTRATED BY

Leonard Everett Fisher

BENCHMARK BOOKS

MARSHALL CAVENDISH
NEW YORK

Benchmark Books
Marshall Cavendish Corporation
99 White Plains Road
Tarrytown, New York 10591

Library of Congress Cataloging-in-Publication Data
Fisher, Leonard Everett.
The weavers / written and illustrated by Leonard Everett Fisher.
p.   cm. — (Colonial craftsmen)
Includes index.
Summary: Presents background information on cloth making in the colonies
and describes the various techniques involved..
ISBN 0-7614-0509-7 (lib. bdg.)
1. Hand weaving—United States—History—Juvenile literature. 2. Weaving—United
States—History—Juvenile literature. [1. Hand weaving—History. 2. Weaving—History.
3.United States—History—Colonial period, ca. 1600–1775.]
I. Title. II. Series: Fisher, Leonard Everett. Colonial craftsmen.
TT848.F55 1998 677'.028242'097409033—dc20 96-36135 CIP AC

Printed and bound in the United States of America

3   5   6   4   2

Other titles in this series

A Short History

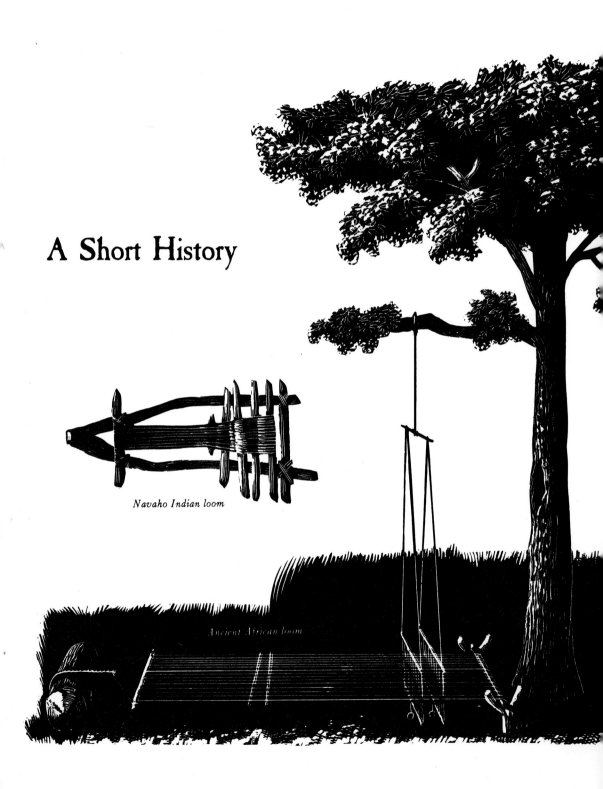

Navaho Indian loom

Ancient African loom

WEAVING IS THE CRAFT OF making cloth by lacing together two sets of thread or yarn at right angles to each other. This is done on a frame called a *loom*. The loom holds very tight, parallel threads called the *warp*, stretching lengthwise away from the weaver. He weaves crosswise parallel threads, called the *woof* or *weft,* from side to side, over and under the warp threads.

The craft of weaving is very old. Nobody is quite sure who the first weavers were or where they lived. People were weaving cloth in the fertile river lands of southwestern Asia almost seven thousand years before the Pilgrims sailed to the New World, and basket weaving is much older than that.

Wonderfully skilled weavers in many parts of the world were busy at their looms, producing plain and luxurious fabrics for a variety of purposes hundreds of years before Christopher Columbus made his first voyage across the Atlantic Ocean in 1492. Long before the first Spanish explorer-adventurers set foot on the beaches of

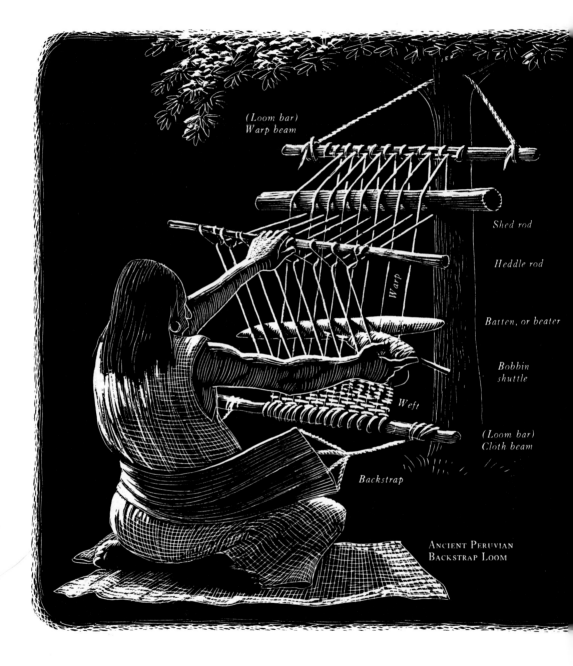

(Loom bar)
Warp beam

Shed rod

Heddle rod

Warp

Batten, or beater

*Bobbin
shuttle*

Weft

*(Loom bar)
Cloth beam*

Backstrap

ANCIENT PERUVIAN
BACKSTRAP LOOM

Ancient Inca woven cotton shirt,
embroidered with wool

the Western Hemisphere, weavers of the great Indian civilizations of Central and South America were making beautifully designed cloth that is still the marvel of all who see it.

Certainly the craft and trade of the weaver were highly developed on the continent of Europe by the time the first English colonists arrived in America. Many of them came with spinning wheels and looms.

Much of the cloth woven in the colonies was made at home by the women, but everyone in the family helped in some way. The older children combed the fiber to be used, and spun it into yarn to be woven, and even the young children could wind the yarn onto spools. During the long winter months when outside chores were few, many a man took his turn at the loom to help make the cloth the family needed.

Some cloth was woven by craftsmen who did not own looms but traveled from house to house and town to town, doing the weaving for families who had looms but did no work on them. These traveling craftsmen were called *journeymen weavers*.

Nearly all the first colonial families grew their own flax, a plant from which they made linen yarn. While some wool was produced in the colonies, the finest wool yarn had to be imported from England. In early America some cotton grew in the South, but most of that needed for weaving was imported by the colonists from Barbados, a British-owned island in the West Indies.

Those families who had no looms either purchased cloth made by their neighbors, imported it from England, or bought it from the few colonial weaving factories that gradually were started. America's first weaving factory was established in 1638 at Rowley, Massachusetts, by Ezekiel Rogers and twenty cloth-making families who came from Yorkshire, England. But even later, when more factories were set up, there were not enough of them to make America an important weaving center like England or France.

Between 1620 and 1700, England had little reason to worry about American cloth production. In 1700, however, things began to change. No longer were there only a handful of American pioneers struggling against hostile Indians and thick forests. Now 250,000 English colonists were living along the eastern coast of North America. Thousands more settlers were arriving, bringing with them all the skills and knowledge gained over the centuries in Europe.

By 1700, England began to realize that the industry of America's highly skilled craftsmen could someday threaten her control over her colonies. If the colonists could make everything they needed, and more, they would not need England or English goods. England therefore decided to start restricting the amount of goods made, sold, and shipped in and out of her American colonies. These restrictions were forced upon nearly all craftsmen and their products, including the weavers.

England was too far away to be able to enforce the restrictions, however. Before long, some of the journeymen weavers quit traveling and bought looms of their own. They put their wives and children to work spinning and winding yarn while they wove cloth to sell. By 1740 there was enough demand for cloth in the colonies to keep non-traveling weavers busy. Instead of selling their product directly to the people, they sold it to textile merchants, who in turn supplied the weavers with yarn. The merchants sold the cloth to tailors or housewives or whoever else needed it.

For the next forty-three years, until the end of the War for Independence, American cloth was made for American use by housewives, journey-man weavers, stay-at-home weavers, and small factories. While the simple cloth products of the American weavers were not as luxurious as those made in other parts of the world, they were just as sturdy and durable, if not more so. They had to be strong to withstand the hard wear de-manded by life in a young, rough, still-growing country.

The colonists got much of the everyday cloth they needed from their own craftsmen, men and women alike. Those who could afford to bought their rich silks and satins from European mer-chants. By the time independence from England came, America had at least some beginnings of the cloth industry that would develop so impor-tantly later.

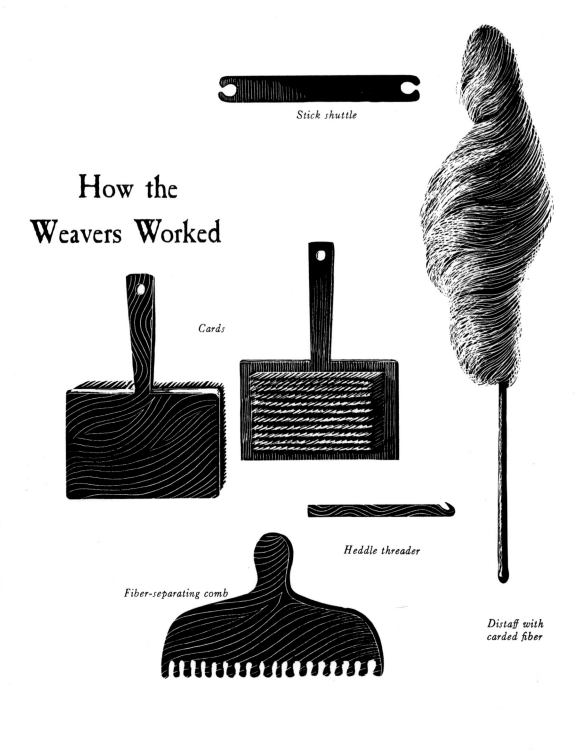

Stick shuttle

How the Weavers Worked

Cards

Heddle threader

Fiber-separating comb

Distaff with
carded fiber

NO MATTER HOW SKILLFUL A weaver was, the cloth he made was only as good as the thread or yarn it was woven from. Some ready-made yarn such as that spun of fine wool was imported from England. Usually, however, the weaver had to make his own yarn — of wool from the sheep he raised, of linen from the flax fibers he grew himself, or from the raw cotton that came from Barbados.

In order to make good yarn properly, the weaver and the entire family first cleaned the flax, cotton, or wool fibers. All the seeds, dirt, and other impurities were removed. Next, the fibers were *carded*, or, if they were flax, were *hackled* — straightened by using wire brushes. The short fibers were *combed*, or separated from the long fibers. Then the cleaned, carded, and combed fibers were rolled onto a rod called a *distaff*. Since this rolling was usually a job for colonial women, they were often called the distaff side of the family.

Next, the slender single fibers on the distaff had to be made into thread or yarn of the thickness desired. This was done by attaching the necessary number of fibers to a rod called a *spindle,* and twisting them together by rotating the spindle. To do this, the distaff with its supply of fiber was placed on a *spinning wheel.* The most popular spinning wheel used in colonial America was the Saxony, or German, wheel. It stretched, twisted, and wound the yarn.

The entire spinning wheel was about as big as an oversized chair. It had a large drive wheel fixed between two upright posts at one end of a slab of wood supported by three legs. At the

Distaff with carded fiber

SAXONY SPINNING WHEEL

*Drive
wheel*

*Drive
belts*

Pulleys

FLYER

*Distaff
with yarn*

*Drive
belts*

Treadle

LEF

other end of the slab, set between two smaller posts, was a hollow spool, or *bobbin*, attached to a small grooved wheel called a *pulley*. A shaft, or *spindle,* passed horizontally through the bobbin and was joined to the two smaller posts.

At one end of the horizontal spindle shaft was another, larger pulley. Attached to the other end of the spindle shaft was a piece of wood curved like the letter U. This was called a *flyer*. Together with the spindle it twisted the fibers into thread, and it also held the spun thread so that it would wind evenly on the bobbin.

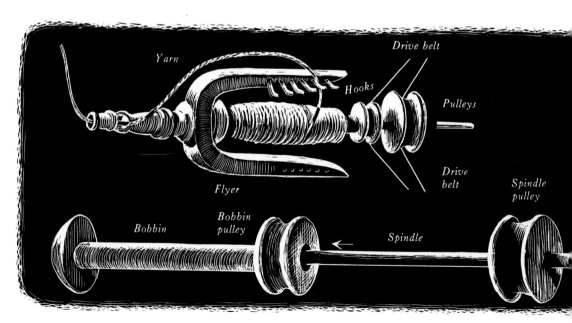

Cords called *drive belts* were looped around the drive wheel and both pulleys. Located under the spinning wheel's slab of wood was a foot lever, or *treadle*, which was connected to the drive wheel by a rod, or arm.

When everything was ready, the spinner pulled a length of fiber from the distaff and pushed it first through an eye in the spindle tip, then around one of a series of hooks at one end of the flyer. From there the fiber was pulled downward and attached to the bobbin.

The spinner then began to work the treadle, making the large drive wheel turn. This moved the drive belts, which then set the two pulleys in motion. The large pulley turned the spindle with its flyer, which twisted the fiber as the person who was spinning pulled it from the distaff. The small pulley turned the bobbin, which wound up the newly spun yarn fed to it by the flyer. Because the small pulley turned faster than the large pulley, the bobbin was able to wind the yarn tightly as the flyer on its spindle twisted it. Every once in a while the person who was spinning moved the thread to a different hook on the

The *TECHNIQUE*

flyer, so that the thread would wind evenly on the bobbin.

The warp yarn was usually spun first, since no weaving could be done until the warp threads had been stretched as tightly as possible from the back to the front of the loom. These threads had to be very strong. In colonial times they were made of linen yarn because the colonial weavers were unable to spin strong enough warp threads out of any other fiber.

Once the yarn was spun, it might be used in its natural shade. But if any other color was desired, the yarn was dyed at home — boiled for a long time in a huge iron, copper, or brass kettle. The dull colors for everyday work clothes could be made from natural vegetable materials that grew nearby and that anyone could gather. Walnut hulls, alder bark, or butternut bark were used for brown dye. Green peach leaves, mullein, and yellow oak bark made yellow dye, and other weeds and herbs were used for various other colors.

For more expensive and brighter cloth, dyes could be bought. Indigo made a blue dye; madder made beautiful crimson shades; and cochineal, most costly of·all, produced a bright scarlet.

Once the warp yarn had been spun, and possibly dyed, it was wound carefully from spools onto a set of pegs, ready to be stretched on the loom.

The very earliest of all weaving was done with the hands only. But by the time the Pilgrims landed at Plymouth, in 1620, cloth was woven on looms that used not only the hands for their operation, but also the feet. The work was done on *foot looms* — looms with foot levers.

The foot looms used by the colonists were large rectangular machines made of a number of upright posts with crossbeams set at exact right angles to them, and with moving parts.

At the back of the usual foot loom, between two uprights, was a large roller called a *warp beam*. The weaver first attached the warp yarn to this beam and rolled some extra yarn around it, to be used later in weaving. He then pulled the warp yarn forward, passing each warp thread through the eye of a *heddle*, which was a loop of cotton or linen cord. The heddles were attached in a row to *heddle bars* — two crossbars, one of

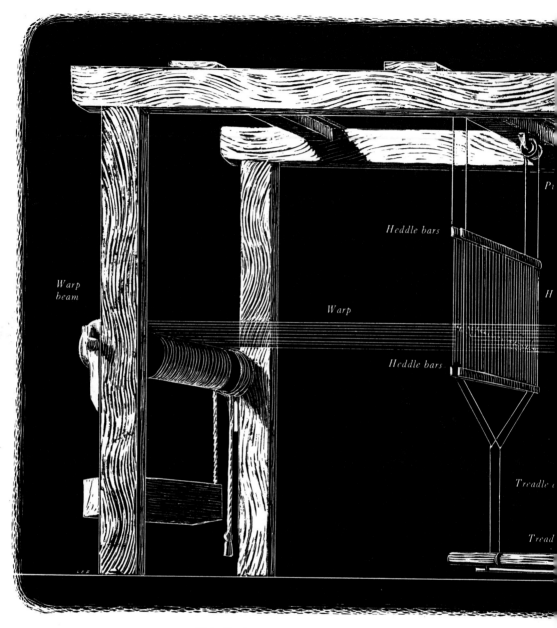

Plain English foot-power loom (also called counterbalanced foot-power loom), typical of the loom used in colonial America.

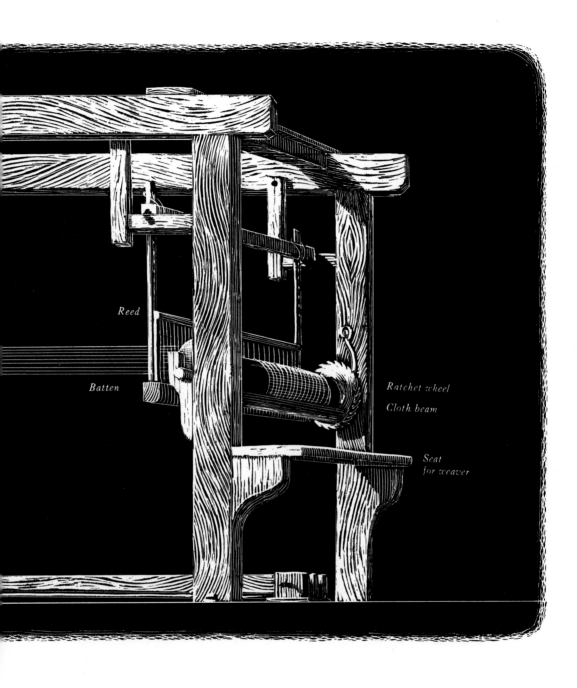

Reed

Batten

Ratchet wheel

Cloth beam

Seat
for weaver

which hung over, and the other under, the warp. The heddles and heddle bars together were called a *harness*. The crossbeams of the harness ran exactly parallel to the warp beam and to the front beam of the loom, and exactly at right angles to the warp threads. It was important that everything on the frame of the loom be exactly parallel or exactly at right angles. If it were not, a crooked piece of cloth would result.

Each loom had at least two harnesses. The bottom crossbar of each harness was connected

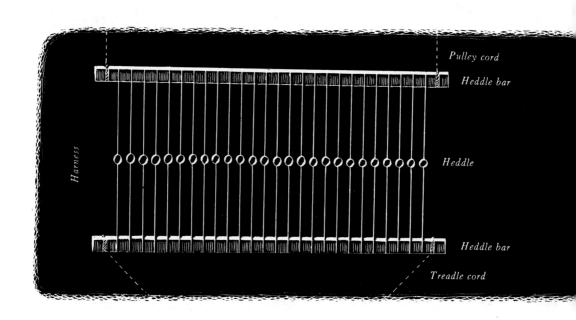

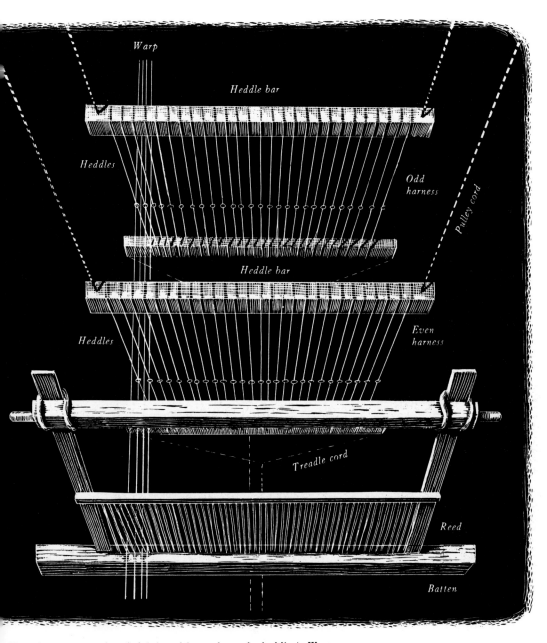

Warp

Heddle bar

Heddles

Odd
harness

Pulley cord

Heddle bar

Heddles

Even
harness

Treadle cord

Reed

Batten

How the warp was threaded (viewed from above the heddles). Warp
threads 1 and 3 pass through the heddle loops of the odd harness;
warp threads 2 and 4 pass through the heddle loops of the even harness;
and so on, according to whether the warp thread is an odd or an even one.

to a treadle, while both top crossbars hung by cords that passed over pulleys at the top of the loom.

To make a plain-woven piece of cloth, the heddles were arranged on two harnesses so that every other warp thread (or the even-numbered threads) passed through the loops of one harness, while the threads in between (or the odd-numbered threads) passed through the loops of the other harness. In more complicated weaves, more harnesses were used.

Once each one of the warp threads had been passed through the correct heddle, the weaver then pulled it through a *reed*, which looked something like a wooden comb. Sometimes each of the warp threads passed through a single opening in the reed, which swung from the top of the loom in front of the harnesses and was weighted by a heavy crossbar below the warp. Sometimes more than one thread passed through a reed opening. After the threads had been passed through the reed they were then tied to another roller, called a *cloth beam*. Next, the warp thread was stretched as tight as possible by rolling back the warp beam. Sometimes the weaver pushed two sticks through the warp, halfway between the harnesses and the warp beam, to keep the warp from tangling.

Preparing the warp on the loom was a slow and tiresome job. It was most important that each warp thread be passed through the correct heddle and reed slots. Otherwise, an imperfect piece of cloth would be woven. If, when the warp had been tightened, the weaver found that a mistake had been made in threading a heddle or a reed slot, the warp had to be removed up to that place, and then rethreaded from that point on.

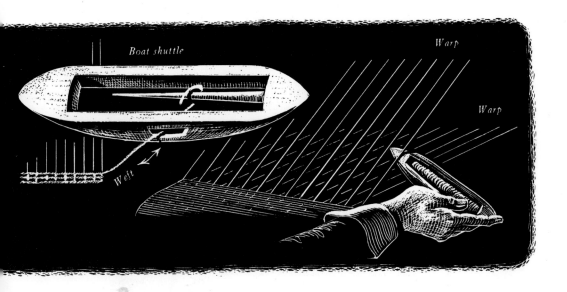

When a shed is made between the odd-numbered and even-numbered warp threads, the shuttle holding the weft is thrown through by the weaver.

Once the warp was correctly in place, the weaver, often a woman, prepared the thread for the weft. She rolled it on a spool, or *quill*, which she placed in a smooth wooden holder called a *shuttle*, which was often made of applewood or boxwood. The end of the weft thread was passed through a hole in the side of the shuttle. Now the weaver was ready to weave.

In order to do this, she had to pass, or *throw*, the weft, or crosswise yarn, back and forth, over and under the threads of the warp. She pressed a treadle with her foot. This raised one harness and lowered the other. Let's say it *raised* the harness with the even-numbered warp threads and *lowered* the harness with the odd-numbered warp threads. The space, or *shed*, made between the two sets of threads in this way was enough to allow the weaver to throw the shuttle and its yarn through.

When the shuttle had been thrown from one side of the warp to the other, the weaver eased the pressure of her foot on the first treadle and stepped on the second treadle. Now she *lowered* the even-numbered threads and *raised* the odd-numbered threads. This was the opposite of what

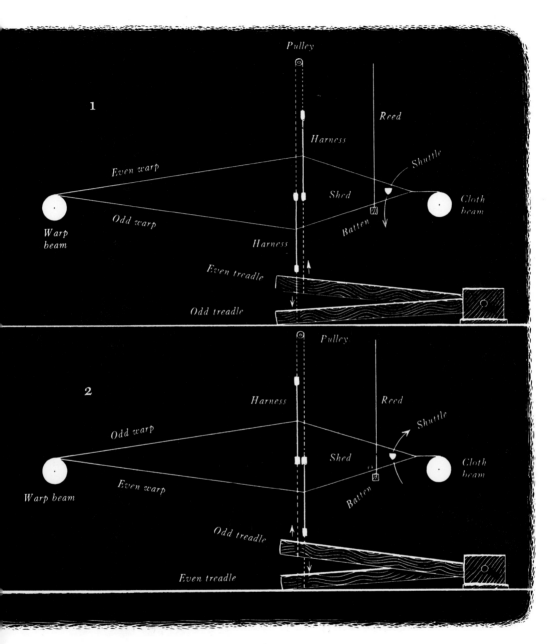

*A cross-section diagram of a loom, showing (1)
the even-numbered warp threads raised and
the odd-numbered warp threads lowered,
and (2) the odd-numbered warp threads raised
and the even-numbered warp threads lowered.*

had happened to the warp the first time she had pressed a treadle. Now she threw the shuttle back, and took the pressure off the treadles, returning the warp to its original position, without a shed. Two lines of weft had been woven into the warp. The first line of weft passed *under* every even thread of warp and *over* every odd thread. The second line of weft did just the opposite, passing *over* every even warp thread and *under* every odd one.

Next, the weaver swung the heavy reed forward against the lines of weft, to press, or *batten*, them closely together. When the shuttle had been thrown back and forth enough times and the weft had been battened, the weaver rolled the finished material forward onto the cloth beam and continued weaving the length of cloth on the new warp brought forward from the rear warp beam.

The weft was one continuous length of yarn. If the yarn broke or was too short, or if its color and thickness were changed because the weaver was following a design, the next length was tied to it with a *weaver's knot*. The weft had to be strong enough not to break. It had to be long

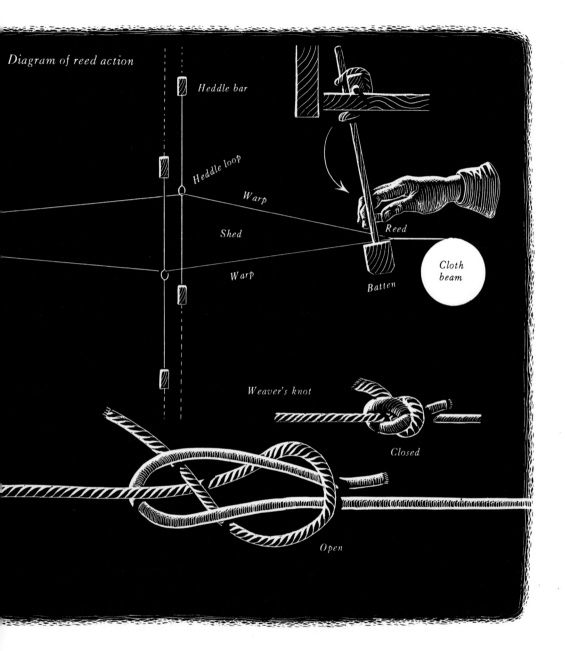

Diagram of reed action

Heddle bar

Heddle loop

Warp

Shed

Warp

Reed

Batten

Cloth beam

Weaver's knot

Closed

Open

*Although this sampler was made in 1789,
it is similar to others
made in late colonial times.*

The *TECHNIQUE*

enough to stretch back and forth between the warp beams and the cloth beams with as little knotting as possible. The edges of the warp, where the weft was turned to be woven back across the width, were called *selvages*. The selvage on each side of the entire length of warp kept the cloth from coming apart.

Passing the weft over and under and then under and over every even- and odd-numbered warp thread made a *plain weave*. The plain weave was one of three weaves from which came all weaving patterns. The other two weaves were the *twill weave* and the *satin weave*.

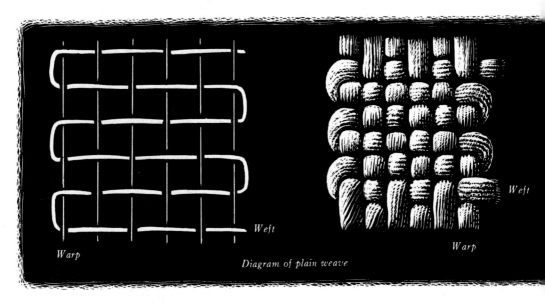

Weft

Weft

Warp

Warp

Diagram of plain weave

The plain weave was the most popular one in the colonies. Many fine cloths for shirts and napkins were plainwoven. Rough cloths were also plainwoven and were used for such things as *samplers*, those pieces of needlework embroidered with names, dates, alphabets, pictures, and maxims. Plainwoven cloths were the best for stamping with inked woodblocks carved with designs, to make printed fabrics. The most common plainwoven fabrics made by colonial weavers were *dimity*, a light, corded cloth, and *fustian*, a rough cloth of linen and cotton. The colonists also used plain weaving for another rough cloth, using linen for the warp, and wool for the weft. It was called *linsey-woolsey*.

The *twill weave* made a diagonal pattern in the cloth. It was made by first passing the weft under one and over two or more warp threads in one direction, and then by stepping the over-and-under design so that the weave of the cloth went forward one or more spaces to the right or left diagonally. To do this, more than two harnesses were needed on the loom.

The *satin weave* was also a diagonal weave, although that was hardly noticeable in the cloth.

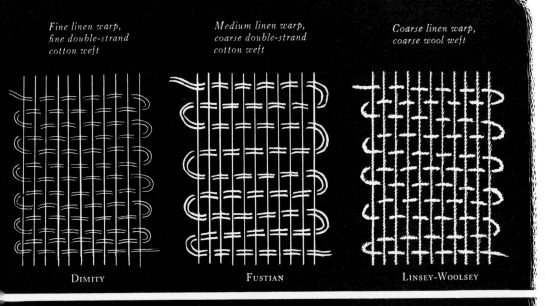

*Fine linen warp,
fine double-strand
cotton weft*

*Medium linen warp,
coarse double-strand
cotton weft*

*Coarse linen warp,
coarse wool weft*

DIMITY

FUSTIAN

LINSEY-WOOLSEY

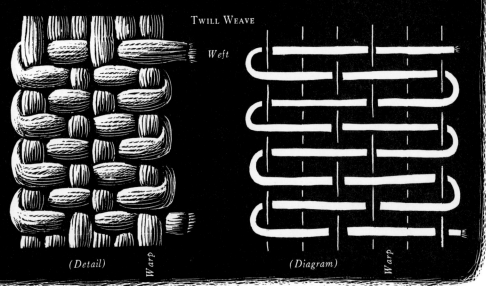

TWILL WEAVE

Weft

(Detail) *Warp*

(Diagram) *Warp*

In this weave the weft passed, or *floated*, over so many threads of warp before passing under one thread that the front and back seemed perfectly smooth. The front of the cloth appeared to be all weft. The back of the cloth seemed to be all warp.

From the simple weaves a great variety of pattern weaves were made with many colors and thicknesses of yarn. Two of the pattern weaves were the *summer-and-winter weave* and the *overshot weave*. To make many of the colonial

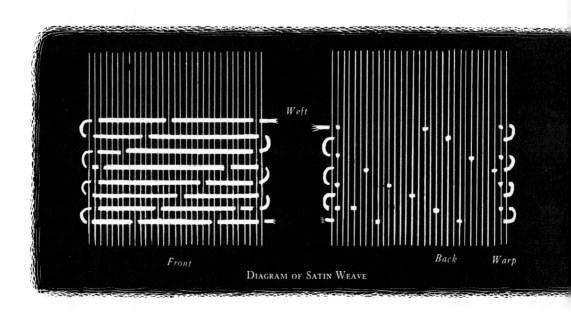

DIAGRAM OF SATIN WEAVE

SUMMER-AND-WINTER PATTERN WEAVE

Wheel of Fortune Pattern

Front   *Back*

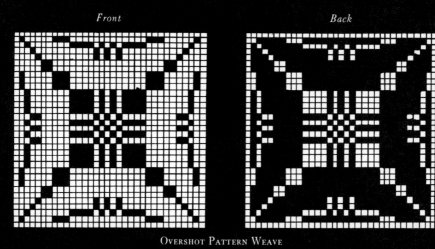

OVERSHOT PATTERN WEAVE

Chariot Wheel pattern   *Indian War pattern*

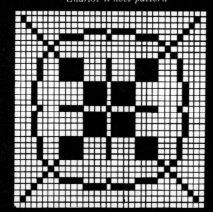 

To weave an overshot pattern, the weaver used two shuttles.
One shuttle was used to plain weave the fabric background.
The other shuttle was used to weave the pattern by skipping or
"overshooting" some of the plain weave warps with a heavier thread.

The summer-and-winter weave was an overshot weave with short, regular
skips over the warp. The weft used to weave the background passed over
one and under three warp threads. The weft used to weave the pattern
passed under one and over three warp threads. As a result, the two
faces of the fabric showed opposite effects in pattern and background.

pattern weaves, four harnesses and treadles were needed on the loom.

Fabrics made in the colonial pattern weaves were decorative. They looked like brocades, cloths in which handsome designs are woven to give the appearance of embroidered cloths. Using the overshot weaves, colonial craftsmen made practical yet decorative bedspreads or coverlets and other such household fabrics. Some of the old patterns have names like poetry: "Blooming Leaf," "Governor's Garden," "Chariot Wheel," "Wheel and Star," "Job's Perplexity," "Indian War," "Queen's Delight," "Wheel of Fortune."

The plans for the weaving patterns could be written out on staves, and were jotted down and passed along from one weaver to another. They looked almost like music, and they meant very little to a non-weaver, but a true craftsman could follow them easily.

Until 1733, all cloth woven in the colonies was not more than thirty inches wide. This was as far as a single weaver could throw the shuttle from one hand to the other. To make a wider cloth, two weavers would have had to throw the shuttle back and forth to each other. It would have been

Blooming Leaf pattern

Modern

pattern draft

Black = weft

White = warp

*Early heddle-threading drafts
for a four-harness pattern.*

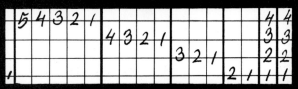

*The first row of numbers
and the horizontal lines
indicate each harness.*

*These numbers and the vertical
spaces indicate the warp
to be threaded on each harness.*

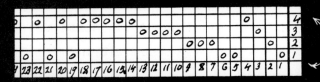

*The first row of these numbers
and the horizontal spaces
indicate each harness.*

*The "o"'s and the vertical spaces indicate the heddles
to be threaded. The numbers at the bottom indicate
each warp thread.*

*Modern heddle-threading draft
for a four-harness pattern*

Black = warp

White = weft

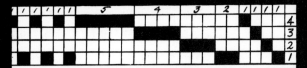

a clumsy way of doing things, and no one bothered to try.

In 1733, John Kay, an Englishman, invented the *flying shuttle*. Instead of throwing the shuttle, the weaver yanked a cord, making the shuttle, equipped with small wheels, roll at high speed across the warp. Although it was a long time before anyone really used Kay's invention, still it did open the way for a single weaver to make cloth wider than thirty inches, and to do it quickly. The flying shuttle marked the beginning of modern automatic weaving machinery.

Most of the American weavers, however, used the old-fashioned foot-powered loom for some time after they became independent American citizens in 1783. They continued to make samplers and coverlets, embroidering and weaving into them eagles, stars, and the motto, "E Pluribus Unum," all proud symbols of a free nation and free individuals. A great deal of their work was so well made that it is treasured today for its quality and as a reminder that modern America was fashioned by craftsmen who used their skillful hands to insure their independence and ours.

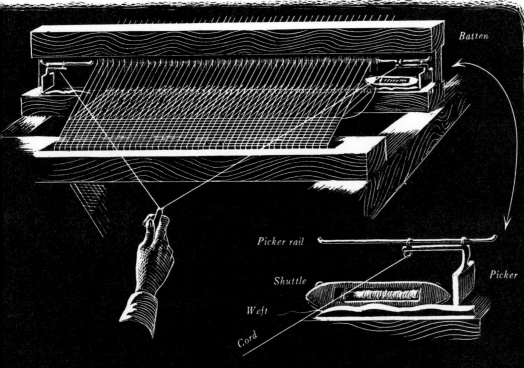

Batten

Picker rail

Shuttle

Weft

Cord

Picker

HE FLYING SHUTTLE

Cord is connected to two pickers, or hammers, mounted on rails located on each side of the loom.

Weaver yanks the cord.

Cord pulls picker.

Picker strikes shuttle.

Shuttle rolls to other side of loom.

At other side of loom, shuttle strikes second picker and settles into a groove which stops it from rolling back until the weaver is ready to yank the cord.

Shuttle

Bottom view

Weft

Top view

Weft

Weavers' Terms

Bobbin — A hollow spool attached to a spinning wheel, onto which spun fibers were wound.

Carding — The process of using a wire brush to straighten fibers for spinning into thread.

Cloth Beam — A roller at the front of the loom to which the warp was attached after having been threaded through the heddles.

Combing — The process of separating the long fibers from the short fibers, for spinning into thread.

Distaff — A rod onto which fibers were rolled before spinning.

Flyer — A U-shaped piece of wood attached to a spinning wheel which aided in spinning the thread and in winding it onto the bobbin.

Foot Loom — A loom operated by the use of foot levers.

Hackling — The process of using a wire brush to straighten linen fibers for spinning into thread.

Harness — The heddles and heddle bars together.

Heddle — A loop of cord through which warp threads were passed, to be raised or lowered in a definite order, according to the weave to be made.

Heddle Bars — The crossbars on the loom to which the heddles were attached.

Loom — A frame on which parallel threads are stretched and other threads interwoven at right angles to make a fabric.

Overshot Weave — A double weave, using more than one shuttle, in which the background was plain woven, and the pattern was made by skipping, or "overshooting," some of the plain-weave warps.

PLAIN WEAVE — A weave made by passing the weft over and under, then under and over, every alternate warp thread.

QUILL — The spool placed within a shuttle to hold the weft yarn.

REED — A device something like a comb, attached to the loom and used to press the threads of the weft evenly together and to keep the width of the woven fabric always the same.

SATIN WEAVE — A diagonal weave in which the weft passes over many warp threads on the face of the cloth before passing under one on the reverse, so making a smooth-looking fabric.

SELVAGE — The edges of the fabric where the weft thread is turned on the warp to be woven back across the width.

SHED — The space between two or more separated sets of warp threads, through which the weaver passes the shuttle.

SHUTTLE — The wooden device used to hold the weft yarn as it is interwoven with the warp.

SPINDLE — The rotating rod that holds the bobbin on which newly spun yarn is wound.

SUMMER-AND-WINTER WEAVE — A double weave which resulted in the effect on the face of the fabric being a reverse of that on the back.

TWILL WEAVE — A stepped weave that resulted in a diagonally patterned fabric.

WARP — The loom yarn stretching lengthwise away from the weaver.

WARP BEAM — A large roller at the back of the loom to which the warp yarn was attached before threading the loom.

WEFT, OR WOOF — The side-to-side yarn which the weaver passes over and under the warp threads on a loom.

Index

Batten, 30
Bobbin, 18, 19-20

Carding, 15
Children, help in weaving, 10, 12
Cloth beam, 26, 30, 32
Combing, 15
Cotton, 11, 15

Diagonal weave, 34
Dimity, 34
Distaff, 15, 16, 19
Drive belts, 19
Drive wheel, 16, 19
Dyeing, 20
Dyes, colonial, 20
  blue, 20
  brown, 20
  crimson, 20
  scarlet, 21
  yellow, 20

Even-numbered warp threads, 28, 30, 32

Factories, early weaving, 11
Fibers, 15-16, 18, 19
Flax, 11, 15
Floating, 36
Flyer, 18, 19-20
Flying shuttle, 40
Foot looms, 21; *see also* Looms
Fustian, 34

Hackling, 15
Harness, 24, 26, 27, 28, 34
Heddle bars, 24
Heddles, 21, 24, 26, 27

Journeymen weavers, 10, 12, 13

Kay, John, 40

Linen yarn, 11, 15, 20, 34
Linsey-woolsey, 34
Loom, 7, 21-27

Merchants, textile, 13

Names, pattern, 38

Odd-numbered warp threads, 28, 30, 32
Overshot weave, 36, 38

Pattern plans, 38, 39
Pattern weaves, 36-39
Plain weave, 32, 34
Printed fabrics, 34
Pulley, spinning-wheel, 18, 19
Pulleys, loom, 26

Quill, 28

Reed, 26, 27, 30
Rogers, Ezekiel, 11
Rowley, Massachusetts, 11

Samplers, 34, 35
Satin weave, 32, 34, 36
Saxony spinning wheel, 16, 18-20
Selvages, 32
Shed, 28, 30
Shuttle, 28, 30, 38, 40
Spindle, 16, 18, 19
Spinning, 10, 16, 18-20
Spinning wheel, 16, 18-20
Summer-and-winter weave, *opp. title page*, 36

Thread; *see* Yarn
Throwing, 28, 30
Treadle, 19, 26, 28, 30
Twill weave, 32, 34

Warp, 7, 20, 21, 24, 26-27, 28, 30, 32, 34, 26
Warp beam, 21, 24, 30, 32
Weaver's knot, 30
Weaving
  in colonial homes, 10, 12, 13
  definition of, 7
  history of, 7, 10-13
Weft, 7, 28, 30, 32, 34, 36
Wheel of Fortune pattern, *opp. title page*, 37
Width of cloth, 38, 40
Woof; *see* Weft
Wool yarn, 11, 15, 34

Yarn, 7, 11, 15, 19, 20, 21, 30

45

LEONARD EVERETT FISHER is a well-known author-artist whose books include *Alphabet Art, The Great Wall of China, The Tower of London, Marie Curie, Jason and the Golden Fleece, The Olympians, The ABC Exhibit, Sailboat Lost,* and many others.

Often honored for his contribution to children's literature, Mr. Fisher was the recipient of the 1989 Nonfiction Award presented by the *Washington Post* and the Children's Book Guild of Washington for the body of an author's work. In 1991, he received both the Catholic Library Association's Regina Medal and the University of Minnesota's Kerlan Award for the entire body of his work. Leonard Everett Fisher lives in Westport, Connecticut.